WAR
DOGS

Kathryn Selbert

ini Charlesbridge

To my father, who would laugh.

Thanks to my mother, brothers, and the Liotta family, as well as RISD admissions, Carol, Judy Sue, Stacy, and Scott P.

Published by Charlesbridge
85 Main Street
Watertown, MA 02472
(617) 926-0329
www.charlesbridge.com

Library of Congress Cataloging-in-Publication Data
Selbert, Kathryn.
    War dogs : Churchill and Rufus: / Kathryn Selbert.
        p. cm.
    Includes bibliographical references.
    ISBN 978-1-58089-414-2 (reinforced for library use)
1. Churchill, Winston, 1874–1965—Juvenile literature. 2. World War,
1939–1945—Great Britain—Juvenile literature. 3. Great Britain—History—
George VI, 1936–1952—Juvenile literature. 4. Dogs—Great Britain—
Juvenile literature. I. Title.
DA566.9.C5S384 2013
941.084092'9—dc23   2012000794

Printed in China
(hc) 10 9 8 7 6 5 4 3 2 1

Illustrations done in acrylic and collage on Bainbridge cold-press paper
Display type set in Toronto Gothic by E-phemera
    and Urgent Telegram AOE by Astigmatic
Text type set in Goudy Old Style
Color separations by KHL Chroma Graphics, Singapore
Printed September 2012 by 1010 Printing International Limited in
    Huizhou, Guangdong, China
Production supervision by Brian G. Walker
Designed by Whitney Leader-Picone

Rufus's best friend, Winston Churchill, is a busy man, but most days Rufus and Winston share a walk.

When it's time for Winston to work, Rufus's ear twitches as he listens to the prime minister's favorite fountain pen scratching furiously. Winston rejects his blunders and blotches, and sheets of paper flutter to the floor like pigeons landing in the park. Rufus sniffs each page.

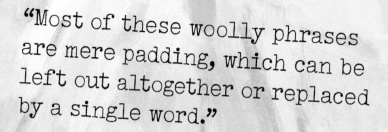

"Most of these woolly phrases are mere padding, which can be left out altogether or replaced by a single word."

—August 1940

When Rufus gets restless Winston leans back in his chair and tells him about the day's events. World War II has recently begun, so there's a lot to say. England, their home, is one of the many countries at war.

Rufus settles down at Winston's feet.

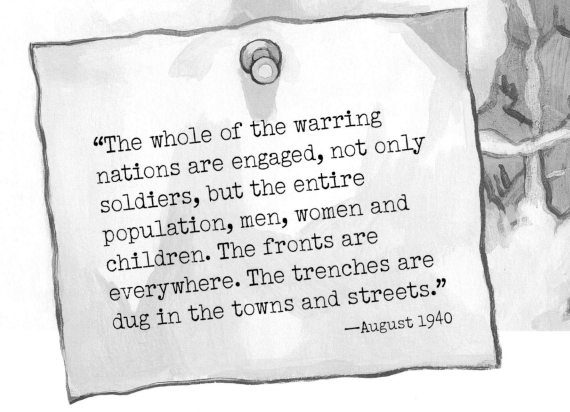

"The whole of the warring nations are engaged, not only soldiers, but the entire population, men, women and children. The fronts are everywhere. The trenches are dug in the towns and streets."

—August 1940

"The road to victory may not be so long as we expect. But we have no right to count upon this. Be it long or short, rough or smooth, we mean to reach our journey's end."

—August 1940

Every day they visit Winston's secret office, hidden beneath the buildings of London. Messages chatter through typewriters, and candy-colored phones rattle and ring. News arrives from all corners of the globe. Rufus explores the nooks and crannies of the bunker, inspecting the kitchen and tiny bedrooms set aside for the people who live and work there.

Clementine, Winston's wife, visits often, holding her husband's hand and kissing his cheek for good luck. She knows that Winston despises the underground bunker and prefers to be outside—even though there are no thick concrete walls to keep him safe.

Rufus jumps into Clementine's lap, begging for treats from the deep pockets of her coat. She rubs behind his ears until he falls asleep.

"This is the room from which I will direct the war."

—circa 1940

"Almost a year has passed since the war began, and it is natural for us, I think, to pause on our journey at this milestone and survey the dark, wide field."

—August 1940

One afternoon Winston gathers his papers, and he and Rufus hurry to the House of Commons. A sea of people settle onto the green velvet benches, waiting for news about the war.

Winston, his shoulders set like a tenacious bulldog's, wades to the front of the hall and begins to speak. Rufus looks on attentively, his tail drumming against the seat back.

Back in the bunker Winston paces from room to room, Rufus trailing behind. Outside a siren wails and bombs blast. A helmet rests snugly on Winston's head, the strap buckled tightly beneath his chin. Rufus clutches Winston's bowler hat between his teeth. Their home is under attack.

The city smells of fire.

"We shall not fail or falter; we shall not weaken or tire. Neither the sudden shock of battle, nor the long-drawn trials of vigilance and exertion will wear us down."

—February 1941

When the smoke lifts in the morning, Winston pulls off his helmet and reaches for his cane. Eager to be outside, Rufus barks and runs quickly to the door. He and Winston inspect the city. Buildings have collapsed and burned in the night. Bricks and glass cover the roads. The German forces have destroyed much of London. Winston clenches his jaw tight as a bulldog's.

"I confess to you that my heart bled for London and the Londoners."

—July 1941

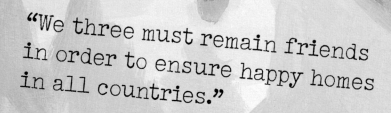

"We three must remain friends in order to ensure happy homes in all countries."

—November 1943

It's soon time for Winston to meet with his allies, Franklin
Roosevelt from America and Joseph Stalin from Russia. Together
they are planning D-day, a great invasion of Normandy, France,
that they hope will lead to the end of the war.

While Winston is gone Rufus sits by the door and carefully
guards the bunker. He waits and waits.

When Winston returns he continues to work doggedly with his advisors and allies to make sure the invasion plans are perfect. When his eyes are tired from planning and plotting, Winston relies on Rufus to keep his spirits up.

"And what a plan! This vast operation is undoubtedly the most complicated and difficult that has ever occurred."

—June 1944

"It involves tides, wind, waves, visibility, both from the air and the sea standpoint, and the combined employment of land, air and sea forces . . ."

—June 1944

In June there is hushed excitement as troops storm across the beaches of Normandy. Rufus stays very still as Winston holds him and points out on the giant map where the soldiers are marching through foamy waters, crossing mountains and beaches, and liberating cities and towns that have been captured by the Germans.

Soon London no longer shakes from the impact of bombs. The invasion of Normandy has been a success. England and its allies have stopped the German forces. The war is ending, and Winston returns to his office in Parliament, where thousands of cheering people line the streets. Winston stands by the window and shouts,

"THIS IS YOUR VICTORY!"

The people roar back, "No! It is yours!"

Rufus barks and howls as all of London sings, sways, and whoops with happiness.

"You have been attacked by a monstrous enemy— but you never flinched or wavered. London, like a great rhinoceros, a great hippopotamus, saying: 'Let them do their worst. London can take it.' London could take anything."

—May 1945

Rufus and Winston share more walks together. Walls that have crumbled from blasts and fire are rebuilt, and the streets are swept clean. London will never be the same as it was, but it experiences a new beginning.

One day, his bags packed and his office cleared out, Winston bundles into his long, woolly coat, pulls on his top hat, and calls to Rufus. Winston switches off the little lamp with a click and softly shuts the door behind them. Winston is no longer needed in the bunker. It's time for a new beginning for him and Rufus.

"Let us go forward together."
—August 1945

Outside, Winston lifts Rufus into a rickety black car. They ramble away from the busy streets. Rufus barks hello to everyone he sees.

They stop outside a large house, where Clementine greets them. She pulls them into a great hug and lets Rufus lick her cheek. Rufus and the man known as the British Bulldog sniff the sweet, fresh air together.

They rest in the country at last, two war dogs.

TIME LINE
of WORLD WAR II

1939

1940

1941

1942

SEPTEMBER
World War II begins, marked by Germany's invasion of Poland. Over the course of the war, the United Kingdom, France, the United States, the Soviet Union, and other countries form the Allied powers, a coalition that opposes Germany, Italy, Japan, and the other countries that constitute the Axis powers.

MAY 10
Winston Churchill replaces Neville Chamberlain as prime minister of Britain. Churchill is considered an unreliable candidate because of his temperamental and idealistic attitude. Germany invades France, Belgium, the Netherlands, and Luxembourg.

JUNE 10
Italy declares war on France and Britain.

JUNE 22
France surrenders and is divided into German- and Italian-controlled territories.

JULY 10
The Battle of Britain begins, during which German forces attempt to gain superiority over the Royal Air Force (RAF) but fail to force Britain to surrender. The battle lasts until October 31.

SEPTEMBER 7
The Blitz, an eight-month-long bombing raid on Britain by German air forces, begins. An estimated 43,000 British civilians are killed.

JUNE 22
German forces begin Operation Barbarossa, in which they attack the Soviet Union. (The Soviet Union comprised Russia and fourteen other small republics that are now independent countries.)

AUGUST 14
Churchill and US president Franklin D. Roosevelt consent to the Atlantic Charter, which outlines their shared ideals and goals for after the war. The United States agrees to protect Atlantic trade routes and lend Britain support.

JANUARY 1
The document Declaration by United Nations is signed by twenty-six nations, uniting them as WWII allies and forming the basis for the modern United Nations. For the duration of the year, the war is fought globally.

DECEMBER 7
Japanese air forces attack Pearl Harbor in Hawaii.

DECEMBER 8
Japanese forces attack the Philippines and Guam. The United States and Britain declare war on Japan.

DECEMBER 11
Germany and Italy declare war on the United States.

1943

JANUARY 14–24
At the Casablanca Conference, Churchill and Roosevelt plan the Allied invasion of Sicily, Italy, in an attempt to force Germany to surrender.

FEBRUARY 2
Over 90,000 German troops surrender to Soviet armies at the Battle of Stalingrad.

JULY 25
Italian dictator Benito Mussolini is overthrown.

JULY 27
Italy's fascist government is dissolved.

SEPTEMBER 3
Troops from the Allied powers join forces in Italy after Sicily is defeated.

SEPTEMBER 10
Germany seizes Rome, Italy.

NOVEMBER 28
Churchill, Roosevelt, and the Soviet leader Joseph Stalin convene for the first time during the war at the Tehran Conference in Iran.

1944

JANUARY 27
The 872-day German blockade of the Soviet city of Leningrad ends.

FEBRUARY 22
Allied powers begin a massive bombing campaign against Germany.

JUNE
US and British troops enter and capture Rome.

JUNE 6
Allied powers launch D-day, or Operation Neptune, an invasion against Germany's forces on the beaches of Normandy, France. The success of the attack leads to the liberation of concentration camps and cities across Europe over the next year.

DECEMBER 16
Germany launches the Battle of the Bulge, a counter-offensive in Belgium.

1945

FEBRUARY 11
Churchill, Roosevelt, and Stalin sign an agreement at the Yalta Conference that establishes the basis for the occupation of Germany and returns lands to the Soviet Union that had been taken by Germany and Japan. The Soviet Union agrees to a friendship pact with China.

APRIL 12
Roosevelt, Churchill's political ally and close friend, passes away.

APRIL 28
Mussolini is captured by Italian anti-fascists and killed in Lombardy, Italy.

MAY 1–2
Germany's dictator, Adolf Hitler, commits suicide, and Berlin falls to the Allied Powers.

MAY 8
Allied powers declare Victory in Europe day (V-E day). This marks the end of the war in Europe.

AUGUST 6
The United States drops the atomic bomb, a nuclear explosive, on Hiroshima, Japan, in an attempt to force Japan to surrender.

AUGUST 8
The Soviet Union declares war on Japan.

AUGUST 9
The United States drops an atomic bomb on Nagasaki, Japan.

SEPTEMBER 2
Japan signs surrender terms aboard the battleship *Missouri*, signaling the end of the international conflict.

OF CHURCHILL AND POODLES

During his lifetime Winston Churchill owned two brown miniature poodles. He named both Rufus. Rufus I (the Rufus in this book) was brownish red and responded to the nickname Paprika. One of Churchill's bodyguards in 1946 testified to having heard the prime minister call forth, "Come, Paprika, let us go forward together," on more than one occasion.

In 1947, after the death of Rufus I in an automobile accident, Churchill was asked if he would like a new breed of dog. He declined, asking instead for another brown miniature poodle. Rufus II became the prime minister's loving companion after WWII.

At Chequers, his country house, Churchill is recalled to have covered Rufus II's eyes while watching an unpleasant scene in *Oliver Twist*, saying, "Don't look now, dear. I'll tell you about it afterwards."

Emma Soames, Churchill's granddaughter, remembered Churchill and his canine friend at the Chartwell estate and family home: "If Grandpa was not at the goldfish pond we would find him there on the lawn, gazing for hours at the rolling view. We would sit near him and 'hold his paw' while avoiding his rather old and fractious poodle, Rufus."

Churchill's love for animals extended beyond his affection for dogs. During his lifetime he had many cats that were beloved and constant companions, and he also enjoyed the company of parakeets and chickens.

THE MAN HIMSELF

Sir Winston Leonard Spencer-Churchill (1874–1965), a politician, artist, orator, and author, is best known for his accomplishments as British prime minister during World War II. Before his time in office, he served in the British Army, including briefly during World War I, and acted as the chief war correspondent for the *Morning Post* during the Boer War.

Serving as prime minister twice (1940–45 and 1951–55), Churchill raised national morale throughout the United Kingdom via his radio addresses to the public. He was an excellent orator, and his radio speeches proved vital in rallying the British people and creating a unified war effort. Churchill was also responsible for creating and nurturing a friendship between the United Kingdom, the United States, and the Soviet Union—a friendship that led to vital war effort support.

Possessing a larger-than-life personality and a brash attitude, the prime minister strongly believed in the destiny of the British people and his place with them. He is well known for his excellent sense of humor and quick wit and is one of the most quoted figures in history.

The title of this book refers to Churchill's long-standing association with the English bulldog. A stubborn champion of his people, he was often called the British Bulldog. (Churchill's wife, Clementine, however, nicknamed him Pug.) Many people mistakenly believe that Churchill owned a bulldog during his lifetime. He was in fact a loving poodle owner.

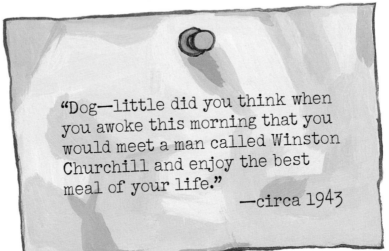

"Dog—little did you think when you awoke this morning that you would meet a man called Winston Churchill and enjoy the best meal of your life."

—circa 1943

BOOKS FOR YOUNG CHURCHILL FANS

Haugen, Brenda. *Winston Churchill: British Soldier, Writer, Statesman*. North Mankato, MN: Compass Point Books, 2006.
    Complete with sidebar "Fast Facts" and detailed photos and illustrations, this biography discusses Winston Churchill's achievements, tenacity, motivations, and more.

MacDonald, Allen. *Horribly Famous: Winston Churchill and His Woeful Wars*. New York: Scholastic, 2009.
    The life of Winston Churchill is conveyed with humor and wit through passages from the prime minister's imagined secret diary and in the book's mock newspaper, *The Winston Weekly*.

MacDonald, Fiona. *Trailblazers of the Modern World: Winston Churchill*. New York: Gareth Stevens Publishing, 2003.
    Read about Churchill's childhood, political career, war years, and personal life in this comprehensive biography.

Wood, Douglas. *Franklin and Winston: A Christmas That Changed the World*. Somerville, MA: Candlewick, 2011.
    Follow the friendship of Churchill and Franklin D. Roosevelt in this picture book that celebrates Churchill's visit to the White House during the Christmas before WWII ended.

CHURCHILL AND WORLD WAR II–RELATED WEBSITES

BBC Primary History: World War 2
http://www.bbc.co.uk/schools/primaryhistory/world_war2
    Complete activities and quizzes and browse archival photos to learn about life in Britain during WWII.

The Churchill Centre and Museum at the Churchill War Rooms, London
http://www.winstonchurchill.org/learn/speeches/speeches-of-winston-churchill
    Search audio clips, video clips, and speeches. Discover truths and myths about Churchill.

The Flying Clippers
http://www.flyingclippers.com
    Trace the development of US military planes and use the site's time line to match the planes with various world events.

Scholastic Student Activities: History Mystery
http://teacher.scholastic.com/histmyst/index.asp
    Professor Carlotta needs help solving WWII mystery questions.

BIBLIOGRAPHY

Addison, Paul. *Churchill on the Home Front, 1900–1955*. London: Pimlico, 1993.

Catherwood, Christopher. *Winston Churchill: The Flawed Genius of World War II*. New York: Penguin Group, 2009.

Churchill, Winston. *Blood, Toil, Tears and Sweat: The Speeches of Winston Churchill*. Edited by David Cannadine. Boston: Houghton Mifflin, 1989.

Churchill, Winston S. *The Churchill War Papers. Vol. 2, Never Surrender; May 1940–December 1940*. Compiled by Martin Gilbert. New York: W. W. Norton, 1994.

——. *The Second World War. Vol. 5, Closing the Ring*. Boston: Houghton Mifflin, 1951.

——. *The Unrelenting Struggle: War Speeches by the Right Honorable Winston S. Churchill*. Compiled by Charles Eade. Boston: Little, Brown and Company, 1942.

——. *Victory: War Speeches by the Right Honorable Winston S. Churchill*. Compiled by Charles Eade. London: Cassell & Co. Ltd., 1946.

——. *Winston S. Churchill: His Complete Speeches 1897–1963. Vol. 6, 1935–1942*. Edited by Robert Rhodes James. New York: Chelsea House Publishers, 1974.

Coombs, David, and Minnie Churchill. *Sir Winston Churchill: His Life and His Paintings*. Philadelphia: Running Press, 2004.

Golding, Ronald. "WSC: The Memories." *Finest Hour*, no. 35 (Spring 1982).

Halsman, Philippe. *Winston Churchill with His Dog, Rufus, in the Gardens of His Chartwell Estate*. Magnum Photos, 1951, photograph. **http://archive.deadcatphoto.com/Magnum_Photos/magnumphotos/Philippe%20Halsman/portrait**.

Holmes, Richard. *Churchill's Bunker: The Cabinet War Rooms and the Culture of Secrecy in Wartime London*. London: Profile Books Ltd. in association with the Imperial War Museum, 2009.

Langworth, Richard, ed. *Churchill by Himself: The Definitive Book of Quotations*. New York: Public Affairs, 2008.

Mason, Herbert. [Image of the Blitz]. *Daily Mail* (London), December 29, 1940, photograph. **http://fivefeetofftheground.blogspot.com/2009/08/lika-som-bartwo-peas-in-pod.html**.

Moran, Charles. *Churchill: Taken from the Diaries of Lord Moran: The Struggle for Survival, 1940–1965*. Boston: Houghton Mifflin, 1966.

National Archives of Canada. Winston S. Churchill Address to the Parliament of Canada. Photograph C-022140, December 30, 1941, photograph.

Nel, Elizabeth. *Winston Churchill by His Personal Secretary: Recollections of the Great Man by a Woman Who Worked for Him*. Bloomington, IN: iUniverse, Inc., 2007.

Soames, Mary. *Winston and Clementine: The Personal Letters of the Churchills*. New York: Houghton Mifflin, 1998.

QUOTATION SOURCES

"Most of these woolly phrases are mere padding, which can be left out altogether or replaced by a single word."
—August 1940

> Churchill, Winston S. *The Churchill War Papers*. Vol. 2, Never Surrender; May 1940–December 1940. Compiled by Martin Gilbert. New York: W. W. Norton, 1994.

"The whole of the warring nations are engaged, not only soldiers, but the entire population, men, women and children. The fronts are everywhere. The trenches are dug in the towns and streets."—August 1940

> Churchill, Winston S. Speech to the House of Commons ("The Few"), August 20, 1940. Parliamentary Debates, Commons, 5th ser.

"The road to victory may not be so long as we expect. But we have no right to count upon this. Be it long or short, rough or smooth, we mean to reach our journey's end."—August 1940

> Langworth, Richard, ed. *Churchill by Himself: The Definitive Book of Quotations*. New York: Public Affairs, 2008.

"This is the room from which I will direct the war."—circa 1940

> Holmes, Richard. *Churchill's Bunker: The Cabinet War Rooms and the Culture of Secrecy in Wartime London*. London: Profile Books Ltd. in association with the Imperial War Museum, 2009.

"Almost a year has passed since the war began, and it is natural for us, I think, to pause on our journey at this milestone and survey the dark, wide field."—August 1940

> Churchill, Winston S. Speech to the House of Commons ("The Few"), August 20, 1940. Parliamentary Debates, Commons, 5th ser.

"We shall not fail or falter; we shall not weaken or tire. Neither the sudden shock of battle, nor the long-drawn trials of vigilance and exertion will wear us down."—February 1941

> Churchill, Winston S. *Winston S. Churchill: His Complete Speeches 1897–1963*. Vol. 6, 1935–1942. Edited by Robert Rhodes James. New York: Chelsea House Publishers, 1974.

"I confess to you that my heart bled for London and the Londoners."—July 1941

> Churchill, Winston S. *The Unrelenting Struggle: War Speeches by the Right Honorable Winston S. Churchill*. Compiled by Charles Eade. Boston: Little, Brown and Company, 1942.

"We three must remain friends in order to ensure happy homes in all countries."—November 1943

> Churchill, Winston S. *The Second World War*. Vol. 5, Closing the Ring. Boston: Houghton Mifflin, 1951.

"And what a plan! This vast operation is undoubtedly the most complicated and difficult that has ever occurred."—June 1944

> Churchill, Winston S. Speech to the House of Commons ("D-day"), June 6, 1944. Parliamentary Debates, Commons, 5th ser.

"It involves tides, wind, waves, visibility, both from the air and the sea standpoint, and the combined employment of land, air and sea forces . . ."—June 1944

> Churchill, Winston S. Speech to the House of Commons ("D-day"), June 6, 1944. Parliamentary Debates, Commons, 5th ser.

"This is your victory!"—May 1945

> Churchill, Winston S. Speech from the balcony of the Ministry of Health in Whitehall, May 8, 1945.

"You have been attacked by a monstrous enemy—but you never flinched or wavered. London, like a great rhinoceros, a great hippopotamus, saying: 'Let them do their worst. London can take it.' London could take anything."—May 1945

> Churchill, Winston S. Speech from the balcony of the Ministry of Health in Whitehall, May 9, 1945.

"Let us go forward together."—August 1945

> Golding, Ronald. "WSC: The Memories." *Finest Hour*, no. 35 (Spring 1982).

"Dog—little did you think when you awoke this morning that you would meet a man called Winston Churchill and enjoy the best meal of your life."—circa 1943

> Cawthorne, Graham. *The Churchill Legend: An Anthology*. London: Cleaver-Hume Press, 1965.